Merry Christmas
1975

FORM
OVER FENCES

By Jane Marshall Dillon

SCHOOL FOR YOUNG RIDERS

FORM OVER FENCES

A Pictorial Critique of Jumping
For Junior Riders

BY

JANE MARSHALL DILLON

DRAWINGS BY PATTY K. RUFFNER

New York

Second ARCO Printing, 1975

Published by ARCO PUBLISHING COMPANY, Inc.,
219 Park Avenue South, New York, N.Y. 10003

Library of Congress Catalog Card Number 72-479
ISBN 0-668-02604-9

Edited and Designed by Eugene V. Connett

Printed in the United States of America

TO

ALL OF THE KEEN YOUNG RIDERS

PAST, PRESENT AND FUTURE

OF

JUNIOR EQUITATION SCHOOL
VIENNA, VIRGINIA.

Acknowledgments

To the following individuals who assisted in various ways in the production of this book, I should like to express my warm appreciation.

FOR TAKING PART IN "PANEL" EVALUATION:

Miss Marion Lee, Staff instructor, Junior Equitation School, and a local judge of DGWS, a division of the National Education Association.

Miss Sherry Lough, Staff instructor, Junior Equitation School, and a holder of a Rating in Riding of the DGWS of the National Education Association.

FOR ACTING IN THE ROLE OF "HORSE SHOW JUDGE" FOR SECTION V:

Miss Fen Kollock, Director and owner of Pegasus Stable, Chevy Chase, Md. Recognized judge AHSA in Hunter Seat Equitation. Chairman elect of the Riding Committee of the DGWS, a branch of the National Education Association.

Mrs. Carol Bailey Miller, Recognized judge AHSA, Hunter Seat Equitation.

FOR HER ENTERTAINING SKETCHES:

Patricia Karig Ruffner, Burke, Virginia.

FOR HIS WONDERFUL COOPERATION AND SKILL IN OBTAINING PHOTOGRAPHS:

Mr. Howard Allen, Allen Studio, Middleburg, Virginia, who took *all* photographs in this book except those otherwise noted.

FOR ASSISTANCE IN SETTING UP PHOTGRAPHIC SCENES AND
OBTAINING SPECIAL SHOTS:

Mr. Homer Heller, Falls Church, Virginia.
Mrs. Maxine Rude, Arlington, Virginia.

FOR PERMISSION TO USE THEIR PHOTOGRAPHS:

Mr. A. L. Waintrob, Budd Studio, New York, N.Y.
Mr. Peter Grant, Washington, D.C.

TO THE FOLLOWING PUPILS OF JUNIOR EQUITATION
SCHOOL WHO SERVED AS THE SUJECTS FOR OUR
PHOTOGRAPHS:

Liza Kahn, Oakton, Virginia.
Susan Bishop, Falls Church, Virginia.
Sally Jones, Arlington, Virginia.
Sherrill Milnor, Starkville, Mississippi.
Randy Dillon, Vienna, Virginia.
Joe Fargis, Vienna, Virginia.
Laurie Kahn, Oakton, Virginia.
Jackie Heller, Falls Church, Virginia.
Nan Wood, Arlington, Virginia.
Sara Willis, Vienna, Virginia.
Ridgely Rider, Falls Church, Virginia.
Claudia Wells, Falls Church, Virginia.
Marion Lee, Vienna, Virginia.
Sherry Lough, Vienna, Virginia.
Judi Triebel, Vienna, Virginia.
Christine Sieminski, Vienna, Virginia.
Jill Ridgely, Vienna, Virginia.
Judy Corcoran, Arlington, Virginia.
Lee Hilts, Vienna, Virginia.
Nancy Hahn, Vienna, Virginia.
Peggy Hahn, Vienna, Virginia.
Mary Lou Walsh, Vienna, Virginia.
Beverly Hink, Vienna, Virginia.
Liz Callar, Vienna, Virginia.
Terry Hink, Vienna, Virginia.
Peak Mason, Arlington, Virginia.
Sara Scheleen, Alexandria, Virginia.
Mary Catherine Willard, Arlington, Virginia.
Nadine Oakley, McLean, Virginia.
Nancy Pinion, Arlington, Virginia.

Contents

FORM
OVER FENCES

CHAPTER 1

Worth More Than a Thousand Words

"What do you want to do in class today?" we sometimes ask our pupils. We know the answer in advance; given a choice the response is the same nearly one hundred percent of the time: "Jump!"

In a section of the country where horses and ponies are of a type suitable for jumping (and sometimes even when they aren't!) to ninety-nine out of one hundred people, jumping is the most exhilarating part of riding. In our area, everybody jumps—a little or a lot. We see all types and styles of jumping: the frequently erratic and sometimes abusive style of the self taught "open jump" rider (Sketch I); the polished and masterful style of our Olympic Team members (Sketch II); the ragged style of the child rider who has "learned with the pony" in her backyard (Sketch III); the smooth elegance of the young rider on her well turned out hunter in the Corinthian Class at the horseshow (Sketch IV)—these, and many other types and styles of jumping are part of the picture.

If we go very far in our jumping, most of us would like to give the best performance we can. And to get this performance, we should understand what we are doing, and why we are doing it.

It helps to have a mental picture of what good jumping looks like.

It helps to have someone stand on the ground and criticize you—many hundreds of times.

It helps to look at countless jumps made by others until your eye can pick out a great deal more than just the fact that a horse is leaping over a fence with a rider on his back.

It helps to analyze and study hundreds of jumping photographs.

It has been said that one picture is worth more than a thousand words. Therefore this book is made up mainly of pictures—instead of words. Since jumping is a broad topic, I shall attempt to present only one very small segment of the whole—the style and form of the rider which best enables the horse to use his body efficiently over the fence. This book is not for the total beginner. In it you will not find "spills and chills" (Sketch V) or even pictures of riders with their feet pointing toward heaven, or "left behind" to such an extent that the legs swing under the horse's chin (Sketch VI). After all, even a beginner at riding could hardly miss the

1

point, so why waste a whole book on the obvious? But for the rider who wants to develop a keen "eye" for good style, this book will, I hope, not only be fun but an asset in bettering his own form.

It takes many hours of practice to develop good style over fences. It also takes many hours of LOOKING just to see what the rider's hands, legs, head and body are doing. The camera helps us in this. At my school one of our favorite rainy day projects is the study and analysis of jumping pictures—sometimes we discuss them for hours on end. With this in mind I am putting together various groups of pictures for you to study.

Except in Photo Section 1, where each picture is used to demonstrate clearly one or more specific faults in jumping technique, the errors are not too glaring. In many instances you may have to look pretty closely to see the mistakes. Test your "eye" on the following pages and perhaps you may be better able to do the same thing when you watch riders in the show ring or out hunting. And when you can spot and evaluate the mistakes of others, you will find it easier to correct your own!

SKETCH I

SKETCH II

3

SKETCH III

SKETCH IV

SKETCH V

SKETCH VI

CHAPTER 2

Why Have Form?

Why bother about form and style in jumping anyway? For one reason only—IN MOST CASES it enables the rider *to get the job done a little better.* "Form" was never developed to make the rider "look pretty." Form in jumping is the ability to have one's body behave in such a way that, without LOSS OF ONE'S OWN SECURITY, ONE MAY CONTROL AND (WHERE DESIRED) STIMULATE THE HORSE AND YET NOT *INTERFERE* WITH THE PHYSICAL EFFORTS OF THE HORSE. (There are times, of course, when you deliberately interfere—but this should never be *over a fence.*)

Jumping form is really no more than observance of common-sense rules. This is why I find it hard to keep from laughing when a rider will tell me: "I'm not interested in all this horsemanship stuff—I just want to be a good rider." What, in heaven's name, does he think good form (or horsemanship) is? Even though, with enough talent and dexterity, one might be able to ride over a fence in almost any position, possibly even standing on the horse's rump (Sketch VII), the horse certainly will not be helped by the bizarre position of the rider.

Think about it this way—an athlete running and jumping on his own feet needs to use his tendons and muscles freely. He still may be able to jump with a papoose strapped to his back (Sketch VIII)—or a load so attached that he feels it the minimum amount. If, however, this load wiggles, twists and kicks him when he is in the air, his ability to jump certainly will not be increased. And if his load manages to jerk his head up and back while he is in the air, or to crash down on his back in landing (Sketch IX), certainly his leap will become less efficient. While all this is so self-evident as to sound ridiculous, there are still people who believe that the horse jumps higher, if the rider, *seated on his back,* tries to "lift" the horse by jerking his head upward, or by making a convulsive movement with his own body (Sketch X). Obviously the person who harbors this idea cannot have given much thought to the laws of gravity, or it would become clear that the rider seated or otherwise attached to the horse, cannot "lift" this animal higher into the air (Sketch XI)! Of course, we all have observed horses who have learned to jump with head jerked up by the rider, giving the

6

appearance of being "lifted," but a moment's serious thought reveals that this is nonsense.

So we might say that form in jumping, like form developed in any other sport—golf, tennis, swimming—is made up of rules that *most of the time will help the situation to come out the best.* And now let's take a look at the details of the form we will seek in the saddle, with a discussion on the "why's" and the "wherefors."

SKETCH VII

SKETCH VIII

SKETCH IX

SKETCH X

SKETCH XI

CHAPTER 3

A Close Look at Form

We have said that "form" in any sport is the observance of general rules that MOST OF THE TIME will work out the most advantageously. So now let's take a close look at *FORM* over the fence itself, and consider the logic of each point. At the same time, we must consider what we want this FORM to accomplish. Remember, we want *security* for the rider, *control* over the horse, and *non-interference* with the physical efforts of the horse. We also want to be in a position to use our aids effectively.

First and foremost, if we are going to be secure, we need a really strong BASE OF SUPPORT—that is, bottom of the whole structure—in this case the lower part of you! For this reason, you drive the heels down. This practice will "ball up" the calf muscles, giving better grip, and will give you a floor from which to spring (this "spring" is another important element of your riding; you will be careful NOT to drive the heel down until the ankle joint is "locked"). Heels up and toes pointing down mean that you have no firm floor under you—notice how frequently the stirrup irons rattle with this type of rider.

Still thinking of security and the ability to control the horse too, you will want a steady leg that acts only when you wish it to. So you must practice keeping a light frictional contact all the way through inner surfaces of thighs, knee bones and upper calves. Don't clench until your muscles quiver and the horse's sides become deadened; close in your legs to give an order, or in an emergency.

And now look at the rider's torso. Just as in any other sport, you will need an active alert position—so don't hunch over and hamper the free use of your arms and hands. Open your chest and incline your torso JUST ENOUGH FORWARD to stay in balance with gravity at all times (more about this later). Arms and hands relate only to control and direction of the horse; NEVER should they be used to gain security on the horse— that is, to hold yourself on. And since they are for *controlling* the horse, they must be able to act entirely independently of the rest of the body— another reason for a secure seat! Arms will function best if allowed to hang naturally to the elbow, and to be bent at the elbow. Because, from the elbow, you wish to obtain a direct, soft line of contact to the horse's mouth, capable of keeping the exact amount of "feel"—or minute weight on the reins and hence the bars of the horse's mouth—that you wish. Fingers and wrists should remain soft—wrists must *never be bent backwards,* robbing hands of elasticity. With a smooth line through from the elbow (this is particularly important at the wrists) to the bit, the horse can understand your conversation with him when you close the fingers, or vibrate the bit in his mouth. Last but not least, let us consider the rider's head. If you ride looking down, almost surely you are going to hump your back and destroy that keen, alert posture you are seeking. Further, if you are looking down, you cannot properly estimate and plan your approach to the next fence. If you look to the side, you throw everything off balance. So look up and look ahead—in jumping, this is of vital importance.

And what about your overall design? There are several things you want to consider. First, you want to sit in such a way that the horse will feel your weight the least—except in very occasional instances. Since his strongest portion is directly behind the withers, it would seem a good idea to place your weight there. Moreover, his center of balance is toward the front—his forehand. If you hung him up on gigantic scales, you would find that his "front half" is a little heavier than the "rear half." This is another reason for sitting forward, so that your weight will coincide with his normal center of balance.

Thinking further about your general design, if you are going to be as undisturbing a "papoose" as possible, you will need to sit in such a way that you are not "propped up" by your horse. *You* too will need to be in balance with gravity, which means that you should be directly BALANCED OVER YOUR OWN FEET, toppling neither forwards nor backwards when you clear the saddle. To sit well and strongly over a fence, you should learn to maintain your position with seat just out of the saddle, stirrup leathers vertical, heels well down, feet on the insides of your irons, legs steady, AT ALL GAITS and over uneven as well as level terrain. Naturally, you realize that this is not a normal way of riding, but it is an exercise to test your ability to stay in balance with your horse and with gravity.

There is one other point you must remember in connection with remaining in balance with your horse. When you run or move faster on your own feet, or on roller skates or on skiis, you instinctively lean further forward, in order to STAY BALANCED. You couldn't run, skate or ski very fast, erect or leaning backwards. In fact, you'd probably fall flat on your back in record time.

On a horse, the fact that he is there under you, and can prop you up, may save you from falling on your back, but what an asinine way to engage in an active sport!

So here are your ten commandments of basic form, holding good on the flat and over fences: (Although there is nothing original to tell you about them as they appear in dozens of texts, still they are an essential framework

Photo by Howard Allen, Middleburg, Va.

PHOTO 1

An exercise to test ability to stay in balance with horse.

on which to hang the mental picture of the form which helps your riding go well.)

1. Head up—eyes up.
2. Shoulders open.
3. Arms hanging to elbow and bent at elbow.
4. Elbow to bit—straight line.
5. Body forward as close to pommel of saddle as possible, with seat clearing the saddle during the jump. Be sure not to thrust your body too far forward on the horse's neck. An imaginary line drawn up from the stirrups should show your "rear" behind your feet, to act as a counter balance.
6. Torso inclined enough forward to keep you balanced over feet, always adjusting to the speed of the horse.
7. Inner surfaces of thigh, knee and upper calf in light frictional contact

13

with the saddle (contact becomes muscular during the jump and usually on last few strides before it).

8. Lower leg slanted back JUST enough to enable stirrup leather to hang straight down, and calves of your legs to close directly behind the girth.

9. Ankles bent so that the soles of your feet are visible to person standing on the ground. This point is much more important than you might think. This correct "break" at the ankle helps keep your knees rolled in, and your feet where they belong—against the inside bars of the stirrup.

10. Feet lying on the *inside of your irons,* tread of the stirrup under (or slightly behind) the balls of your feet, heels down; your toes neither dead parallel to one another nor pointing East and West, but at just about the same angle that they are when you walk (most texts say 20 to 30 degrees, but degrees always confuse me!).

Try to have this mental picture *sink in* until your eye not only takes in the overall design of another rider but so that you automatically distribute your own weight and arrange your body in the same way *without thinking about it.* Only when good form becomes completely automatic will it do you any good.

CHAPTER 4

The Process of Learning to Jump in Good Style

While an instructor would be arrogant to imagine that there is only one way of arriving at a particular end, inevitably each must be convinced that his particular way is the best. He (or she) would have to be a real cynic to act on any other line of thinking.

I shall describe the method which we use at my school step by step. But first I should like to outline a few of our general concepts. Incidentally, while I am presenting this from the point of view of the teacher in connection with his "human pupil," many of the same points hold true in reference to the "horse pupil."

Don't waste time by rushing. Take time and trouble to do each step well before attempting the next.

Never try to "push" a frightened rider. If you will see to it that he has only good experiences, he will get over being frightened in due time. Only when he is confident, can he do his best.

Be practical. Realize the limitations of anyone learning learning to ride and jump.

Don't mount the novice jumping pupil on an unpredictable horse. How could the rider possibly learn to do all that the situation would require at once?

Recognize the fact that it is virtually impossible for a rider to have his hands function as he wishes them to if the bottom of the whole structure is shaky—unless he does so at the expense of the horse's mouth. Require him to develop a strong seat, and legs like rocks before he attempts to maintain contact with the horse's mouth over a fence.

And now for a look at an outline of learning to jump, which we believe makes this process safer and simpler for the rider, and *much* pleasanter for the horse. First of all, practice your jump position on the flat (head up, back hollow, seat just clearing the saddle, your "seat" a counter-balance, inner surfaces of thigh, knee and calf in contact with the saddle, stirrup

SKETCH XII

The Cynical Instructor

SKETCH XIII

Never Push a Frightened Rider

leathers hanging vertical, heels well down, ankle joints "breaking" toward the horse's sides, feet lying on the inside of the irons, tread of stirrup under or just behind the balls of your feet). For a while you will need to steady yourself by holding on to a piece of mane, about half way up the horse's neck. When you thoroughly establish your balance and security—which after all is the purpose of this exercise—you will be able to maintain this position with arms out.

There are several "next" steps, and you can practice them alternately. Set up a simple jump course *without* jumps, and practice, as you approach the standards (which you will ride between), stepping down, closing in your legs, and getting up in jump position a few strides before you reach the standards; stay there for a few strides afterwards. Then let yourself down softly—no thumps. You should do this until the shift from normal position on the flat to the position you wish to maintain over jumps becomes completely effortless and automatic. At about the same time, you can start trotting over a rail that is almost on the ground. At this point, the horse may not change his stride over the rail at all, or he may make a tiny little jump. You should concentrate on maintaining the correct position, seat *just* clearing the saddle, steadying yourself by holding on to a piece of mane. See that your legs do not swing forward, letting you come down with a "plop" on the horse's back! As you find that you can close in your legs and maintain the correct position with seat out of the saddle, you will raise the rail a few inches until it really is a small jump.

At the same stage of the game, cavaletti provides an excellent exercise. In this case, establishing a rhythmic trot, you take your jumping position before the first rail, and maintain it over the five or six rails on the ground; the last rail is raised (and the distance from the preceding rail is increased) very gradually, until it becomes a small jump. This device of practicing jumping from a trot with the aid of cavaletti seems to work particularly well; the regular and even strides which the rails laid out on the ground demand of the horse are conducive to a steady, quiet way of jumping.

The rider should continue to jump only willing, well-schooled horses, and should be *required to catch mane* until he is doing easy little courses up to about 3′ comfortably and maintaining a good design of body. He also should alternate the regular jumping practice over the easy courses of low jumps with riding more difficult "jumpless" courses. Here a course is set up (standards only) with no actual fences to clear, but a more complicated course to follow, requiring an entrance circle and all sorts of changes of direction. The rider should work to maintain even speed of a canter and to get good corners and straight approaches. He should take a jump position on the approach to each poleless "fence" and maintain it for a stride on the "landing" side. This practice gives the rider skill in where and how to make his initial circle on entering a show ring, where to start sighting each fence and where to make the turn for a good approach.

17

In other words, how to plan the ride over the course, giving the horse every break. This type of practice gives the rider invaluable experience in "figuring a course" without jumping the horse to death. Too many times have we seen a horse show class lost because of bad approaches.

The jumping practice and technique which we have discussed thus far is the elementary part. Some individuals may find it best to go on jumping this way indefinitely, letting the reins loop and catching mane to steady themselves over fences, to be sure of sparing the horse's mouth. There are much worse ways of jumping. In fact, a good little elementary rider, putting his or her hands up on the neck at the jump, is not a displeasing sight at all. Quite the contrary. The rider may even have developed considerable style and timing while still at this level. On the other hand, a rider who attempts to maintain contact with his horse's mouth and is left behind, snatching his horse in the mouth, is a miserable sight to behold!

Serious pupils in this sport are generally anxious to carry their technique beyond this elementary level. When they can be reasonably sure that they can move with the horse, without snapping back even if he puts in an outsize fence, and can at the same time maintain a strong secure base of support, they should begin to give up the mane, in all but emergencies. By this time they should have learned to make sufficiently strong thrusts with their own bodies at the takeoff so that catching mane is no longer necessary. They will now try to let their hands swing forward and slide along the sides of the horse's neck, following the gestures of his head, and maintaining contact with his mouth. When successfully done, there will be no *pulling* on the rains. The horse's head and neck will operate perfectly freely, undisturbed by the few ounces of "feel" on the bars of the mouth.

Why is it desirable to be able to retain contact with the horse's mouth? For one thing, even though you are never going to hurt the horse's mouth while jumping with looping reins and holding the mane, you have sacrificed control. Riding thus, it is much easier for the horse to "duck out" when he wishes. When the time comes that you can keep that hairbreadth of "feel," or contact with his mouth, you can *feel* what your horse is going to do a great deal better and can stay more completely in one piece with him.

When you first begin to practice "following" over fences in an effort to eventually maintain contact throughout the jump, you will need a small "crutch," although you have now abandoned your "wheel chair"—the mane. Taking some slight support from the sides of the neck will provide this "crutch" for you. It doesn't matter if you get a little slack in the reins for awhile—this is much to be preferred to reins that are too short. While you are successfully "following" the gesture of the horse's head and neck over fences but taking support from the neck, we say that you are jumping on an intermediate level.

Finally, when you have developed a strong, secure base of support, good timing, and hands that function completely as you direct them to, you can

PHOTO 2

Cavaletti provides an excellent exercise.

PHOTO 3

A good little elementary rider, putting her hands up on the neck at the jump.

begin to practice "following through the air." This means that you will now attempt to keep the reins lightly taut, maintaining a straight line of action from your elbow to the horse's mouth, on the approach to the jump, on the takeoff, the flight and the landing. We consider this "jumping on an advanced level," or "advanced jumping style." You may also hear this jumping technique called "jumping out of hand." To accomplish all this, without supporting yourself on the sides of the neck and at the same time maintaining your position just clear of the saddle with feet and legs in place, requires considerable skill.

We are now talking about the style of riding over fences which does give the horse the best opportunity to use all parts of his body as freely as possible without any loss of control or loss of security on the part of the rider—this, you will remember, is what we said we meant by good form in jumping.

PHOTO SECTION NO. I

The Hint Is Broad

In the following section of photographs we are trying to illustrate specific faults that occur in jumping and to be sure that they are completely clear. We have used jumps of various heights and types that bring out the particular points under discussion. For emphasis, we have in most instances used pictures that are wonderfully bad! Most of the photos in this book are from this year's crop of riders who have been brave enough to let me advertise their worst jumps to the world. One or two faults did not appear in our picture-taking spree this year so in these cases, I dug back into the past. Oddly enough, even after going through hundreds of jumping photos, three faults did not appear in sharp enough focus to serve as illustrations, so these we "staged." Just for fun, try to decide which they are!

Having been so malicious as to flaunt my riders' mistakes to the public, it was agreed to be no more than fair that I resurrect an old "awful" of myself. This I have gallantly done. When you come across a strange figure, obviously from another era, it is I!

I should like to list—and then have you spot and match up—a number of the common pitfalls which prevent one's style over fences from being perfect. In the following section each picture illustrates at least one fault in technique. Most will illustrate several; for example, when the rider "ducks" his head and looks down, almost always other parts of his body get out of position too. (Since most of these photos illustrate more than one fault, there are not as many pictures in this section as there are faults described.) Try to match up the photos that serve as the *best illustration of the particular fault under discussion*. Note all other photos that demonstrate the same fault and state whether the rider is jumping in "elementary," "intermediate," or "advanced" style, according to the definition used in Chapter 4. Comment on anything else that interests you—perhaps the fact that the horse "dangles" its legs over the fence, or perhaps that the overall effect is marred because the rider's coat is too short!

Cover the text below each picture and write down your answers before you look at the "Panel Evaluation." * Check your score against the panel's.

* "Panel" answers were worked out by the Riding Staff of Junior Equitation School, Vienna, Virginia.

There are thirty-two faults listed, so deduct three points if you are in total disagreement with the answers in the book; one and one-half points if about half wrong; one point if one-third wrong, etc. A score of over 90 should be considered excellent; 85 to 90 good. If your grade is below this, your "eye" needs to become keener.

Before starting on the list of "sins" there is a point which I suppose I hardly need to mention: even the most perfect style will not make a "great rider." There is no substitute for good judgment, courage, timing, patience and relaxation. But perfect technique will always *improve* the rider who already has "the spark of genius;" the person who has no great natural flair for riding most assuredly *will ride better* if he is willing to drill until good form becomes second nature. Bearing all this in mind, let us take a look at a few things which most assuredly will *not* enable you to ride better!

1. *Head ducking, with rider looking down.* (As already explained, almost always a number of other "sins" will go along with this one—frequently the back becomes rounded, legs lose their correct grip, etc., in addition to the fact that the rider lessens his ability to get ready for the next fence.

2. *Head ducking, to the side.* The other "sins" that go hand in hand with this one are slightly different from those of number 1. The entire balance becomes "lopsided." On the other hand, you may find a rider who has allowed his balance to become "lopsided" without looking down to the side, and that is another fault in itself.

3. *Rounded back.* This is a most common fault. Frequently, it is coupled with the rider looking down, with pivoting on the knees, and lower leg swinging back. The opposite dilemma in which the rider may find himself, relating to the back, is a general stiffness.

And now, in relation to hands and arms we find a multitude of possible pitfalls, as follows:

4. *Hands and arms that do not "give" enough over the fence,* tying in the horse's head in such a way that he cannot use himself properly during the jump.

5. *Arms that "flip out" at the elbows.* When this occurs, it is unlikely that the rider will maintain a soft, direct line of contact with the horse's mouth.

6. *Hands that tend to "ball up into tight little fists"* thus losing their softness.

7. *Hands that are too high,* breaking the soft straight line of action to the horse's mouth and displacing the bit in the horse's mouth in a way that the rider doesn't intend. This is often a relatively minor "sin." This is the case in the picture that illustrates the particular fault. It becomes a major "sin" when the hands fly up in such a way that the rider finds himself swinging on the horse's mouth.

8. *Hands too low,* breaking the straight line of action to the horse's mouth in a downward direction. Unintentionally, the rider is putting pressure on the bars of the horse's mouth and disturbing the direct line of communication *with* the mouth.

9. *Hands that "break" backwards at the wrist,* thus robbing the rider of any possible elasticity in their use.

10. *Hands that "break" the straight line of action to the horse's mouth by rounding of the wrists.* In this instance, the hands hang over like a puppy begging for bones. (This particular way of carrying the hands goes by the facetious term of "puppy dogging" at our school.) This fault appears less frequently in jumping than on the flat. Hands that "break" in this direction generally are soft hands, but tend to lose contact with the horse's mouth. In the photo which we use as an illustration, you will find this to be true, and that the fault exists to a slight degree only.

11. *Curb rein too tight.* The feel of the horse's mouth over a fence should always be from the snaffle rein—never the curb rein. Remember the curb rein is attached to the shank of the bit, and serves as a lever to cause pressure on the bars of the horse's mouth. Allowing this rein to tighten almost certainly will make the horse fearful of reaching out the head and neck as he must to use his body well over the fence.

12. *Fingers that spread out during the jump*—this often goes along with very soft use of the hands too, but is not desirable as it is an excellent way to sprain or break a finger or two! In addition, most of the time this position of the fingers makes it impossible to maintain contact.

N—O—T—E

Before concluding the faults occurring with the hands, the reader should remember that at a certain stage of the game (the early stage), the rider *must* break the straight line of action during the jump, and catch the horse's mane, allowing the reins to be slack—or else he will abuse the horse's mouth. While this should be considered a fault when the rider has reached an advanced stage (although an infinitely lesser one than catching the horse in the mouth) it cannot be considered a *fault* at all in the elementary jump rider. Similarly, at the intermediate level, we may find some slack in the reins and the rider taking support from the horse's neck. It should be *noted*, but must be expected at the intermediate level.

And, now, let us take a look at the rider's seat—and here I am referring to the "seat" literally, not to the overall style of riding.

13. *Seat too far out of the saddle.* Usually this will go with a leg that is too straight. Ideally, the seat should remain *close to* but clearing the saddle during the jump. Thus it is possible to retain the angles of the leg, utilizing their "springs." In addition, it will enable the rider to remain in a more secure position throughout the jump. Normally, during the jump, the rider's shoulders should remain a little higher than his seat. The only exception to this general rule occurs on a high jump, where the rider actually flattens out on the horse. On the average hunter height jump this is totally unnecessary.

14. *Seat that does not "clear the saddle" during the jump,* but continues to sit. Along with this "sitting," most of the time, although not always, you will find that the rider's lower legs come loose from insufficient weight dropped through the heels into the irons. The legs generally swing either backward or forward.

Next we'll give the legs their working over! When we get to this point, it becomes even more difficult to separate and "pigeon-hole" many of the faults of technique since almost always one involves others previously discussed. In other words, you will have to expect "overlapping" in the following analysis.

15. *Legs that swing forward*—thus destroying the base of support. Almost always the rider who is "left behind" when the horse jumps will find his legs out in front of him.

16. *Legs that swing back.* The rider is much less secure in this position than he is when his feet and legs are firmly under him. In addition, he is totally unable to close in his legs. He has a tendency to "pivot on his knees" in such a way that the lower legs have no real stability. During the landing he is likely to crash down on the horse's back.

17. *"Floating lower leg."* Here the leg may be swinging neither forward nor back, but simply angled out from the knees in such a way that, again,

the rider sacrifices security. The rider is also in a less favorable position to use his legs as aids.

18. *Knees out*—away from the horse's sides. This tendency creates an ineffective leg and usually is accompanied by heels rolled into the horse's sides.

19. *Pivoting on knees.* The rider pinches with the inside of the knees, making no use of the rest of the legs, which may wander almost anywhere!

Feet can be the source of many troubles.

20. *Heels up*—this is, probably, the most obvious and one of the most common of all mistakes of correct form. As explained earlier, when the heels come up, the rider has no strong base of support from which to "step and spring."

21. *Feet on the outside of the stirrups.* When this occurs, the inside of the irons are in a position to hit the horse's sides needlessly. In addition, when the rider's feet are on the outside of the stirrups, there is a tendency to step on the outside of the feet, rolling the knees away from their normal position in light contact with the saddle. And as a result, the base of support becomes less strong and secure.

22. *Insufficient break inwards—toward the horse—at the ankle.* This is almost the same as the fault described in No. 21 and has most of the same bad effects.

23. *Feet shot "home" (through to the instep) in the stirrups.* While he may have complete security, the rider robs himself of his "spring and elasticity."

24. *Feet having toes only on the treads of the stirrups.* Now there will be lots of "spring and elasticity" but the stability of the lower leg is sacrificed.

25. *Feet "East and West."* By this we mean that the rider's toes are pointing in opposite directions. This will move the knees out. Also, if the rider is wearing spurs, he will unintentionally gouge the horse in the sides.

Finally, we have a group of faults that cannot be considered to belong to any one part of the body, and which relate in general to the overall design; most have already been discussed in their integral parts.

26. *Rider tipped too far forward.* Every now and then we will find a rider

who simply slants every part of himself too far forward. It is as if the whole should be viewed from a slightly different angle and all would be well. There are many variations of this, combining many individual faults.

27. *Rider too erect.* Most of the time this results from the rider failing to step down and make the necessary thrust with his body as the speed of the forward movement is accelerated in the take-off of the jump. Generally, this fault will result in the rider being "left behind."

28. *Rider "bracing" in the irons.* This rider usually stiffens both the knee and the ankle joints, and because he is standing in his stirrups, loses his elasticity. In addition, he robs himself of the ability to close in his legs.

29. *Rider correct but stiff overall.* The body may be properly arranged, but stiffness throughout robs it of the "fluid" quality which keeps the whole body soft and resilient. The stiff rider is likely to jar himself and bounce a little on landing. He will be less able to remain "all one piece" with the horse.

30. *"Lopsided."* Entire structure "tilts" to side, throwing everything off balance.

31. *Rider lying down on hands.* Catching the mane for support is permissible and desirable in some cases, but this does not mean that the rider should grab the mane and push down or lie down on his hands. When he does this, he loosens his base of support in most cases; also, he won't be able to see where he is going!

32. *Left behind!* The worst crime of all! By this, we mean that the rider fails to make the necessary thrust with his body as the horse takes off for his fence—or makes it too late or makes it too small. If the rider is quick enough, he will try to remedy the situation by letting the reins slide through his hands, or by catching the mane, so that the end result is no worse than that the rider is bounced around, and perhaps bangs the horse's back. Or it may be considerably worse from the horse's point of view. If he does *not* manage to let the reins go, and lets his weight swing against the horse's mouth, his horse is going to develop an awfully sour attitude about jumping!

And there you have our summary of the most common mistakes in form one is likely to see. Now cover the text and study the photos in this section. Naturally, we have "jumbled up" the order in which the pictures illustrating the faults are arranged, or we would have no test. In other words, you may be sure that the first photo in the section will *not* illustrate the first fault described. List your choices for the *clearest illustrations* of each mistake—first, second and third, where you find several—or perhaps there will be "ties" for first, second, and third. Then compare your answers with those of the panel.

Photo by Howard Allen, Middleburg, Va.

PHOTO 4

Fault 29. *Rider correct but stiff overall.* To me, this is a very interesting photo in that the quality of stiffness will show up in a "still." Look closely at the picture. You really couldn't ask to have everything more perfect "stylewise" for a jump at the "beginning-intermediate" stage. But still it looks "fixed." Several "experts" who had never seen this rider spotted the fault; several others saw nothing wrong. How does it strike you?

Photo by Howard Allen, Middleburg, Va.

PHOTO 5

Fault 12. *Fingers that spread out during the jump.* I am sure that this one was not too hard to tab!

Fault 16. *Legs that swing back.* The rider has let the lower leg slip out of position, but one does get a feeling of "fluid ease" in spite of faults in technique. Everything is very free and very soft, but we would like to see all this combined with a little more stability in the base of support; this, in turn, should enable the rider to maintain soft contact with the horse's mouth throughout the jump. ("Intermediate to advanced" style. Fence is spread and is about 4′ 6″ in height.)

Fault 19. *Pivoting on knees.* (see also photo #7.) The rider is getting most of her grip in her knees and failing to make proper use of the calves of her legs.

Fault 26. *Rider tipped too far forward.* Certainly the rider is tilting too far forward and legs have slipped; there is no contact—but in looking at this particular picture, I have the feeling that this rider will move quickly with her horse, and will in no way interfere with him.

Photo by Howard Allen, Middleburg, Va.

Photo 6

Fault 1. *Head "ducking," with rider looking down.* The rider is looking neither to the right nor to the left but she *is* looking down. She certainly does not give the impression that she will be ready for the next fence, should it be close, or for a quick change of direction on landing, should one be necessary! (The jump is more or less on the elementary level.)

Fault 18. *Knees out.* The rider is jumping a low fence in an elementary style. When she gets her hands off the mane and tries to maintain that strong and steady base of support necessary if the hands are to function freely, she will find the knees rolled out a real liability. Or perhaps we might say that her knees came loose because she is lying on her hands.

Fault 23. *Feet shot "home" (through to the instep) in the stirrups.* (See also photos #9, #18, and #20.) The feet have slipped through until the tread of the stirrup is almost against the heel of the boot. When this occurs, the rider loses elasticity and spring. Keeping the tread of the stirrup about one inch further forward makes a big difference.

Fault 31. *Rider lying down on hands.* We have already seen that as this rider lies on her hands and looks down, her knees come away from the knee roll.

*   *   *

In a number of other photos, it is debatable whether the riders are steadying themselves lightly on the horses' necks, or actually dropping enough weight on their hands and arms to loosen the base of support. Photo #6 is the only case in which I am *convinced* that the particular fault is present.

29

Photo by Howard Allen, Middleburg, Va.

PHOTO 7

Fault 19. *Pivoting on knees.* (see also photo #5.) This is such a common fault that I am surprised we do not find more good illustrations of this point in our collection. I think we might take this photo as the best illustration. Here, as the rider pinches with the knee, she loses all correct base of support, and is relying primarily on balance. With no secure floor from which to "step and spring," she must steady herself and stay on by using her hands as "steadiers." This photo could be considered to demonstrate *bad* intermediate style.

Fault 21. *Feet on the outside of the stirrup.* (See also photo #15.) In this particular case, the feet might be anywhere in the stirrups, as the rider is dropping no weight into them—her feet and lower legs are just appendages, dangling from the knee down, and certainly do not form anything remotely resembling a "floor" under her. As a result, not only is her own security lessened and her ability to use her lower leg nil, but she has a loose piece of iron to bang the horse in the sides.

30

Photo by Howard Allen, Middleburg, Va.

PHOTO 8

Fault 8. *Hands too low.* (see also photo #16) This rider has dropped her shoulders almost level with her seat; consequently her efforts to follow result in dropping her hands and arms and breaking the straight line from bit to elbow downwards. In spite of the fact that her hands are soft and that she is in no way interfering with the horse's efforts, this "dropping" must be considered a fault of technique. ("Intermediate to advanced" style.)

Photo by Howard Allen, Middleburg, Va.

PHOTO 9

Fault 28. *Rider "bracing" in the irons*. This rider provides the perfect illustration of "standing and bracing" with no elasticity possible.

Fault 23. *Feet shot "home" (through to the instep) in the stirrup.* (See also photos #6, #18, and #20.)

Photo by Howard Allen, Middleburg, Va.

PHOTO 10

Fault 7. *Hands that are too high.* This is such a good jumping picture that I would have preferred not to use it in this section. However, it does provide a perfect illustration of the straight line from bit to elbow broken upwards, as the rider attempts to maintain contact and follow the gestures of the horse's head and neck. The rider's over-all design really cannot be faulted otherwise. Observe how well the legs stay exactly where they belong, with heels down, feet on the inside of irons, etc. Do you notice any similarity between the style of the rider in photo #24 and this picture? Correct—it is the same rider. (Rider here is attempting "advanced" style.)

Photo by Howard Allen, Middleburg, Va.

PHOTO 11

Fault 2. *Head "ducking" to the side.* To begin with, this young rider is jumping in elementary style and catching the mane to spare the mouth. At her age (10 years) and stage of riding, that is fine. However, she is helping neither herself nor her pony by looking down and to the side. Nor is she in an advantageous position to get ready for the next fence.

But wouldn't it be nice if most horses would fold the front legs as well as her pony does? (The jump is ridden on an elementary level.)

Photo by Howard Allen, Middleburg, Va.

PHOTO 12

Fault 4. *Hands and arms that do not "give" enough over fences.* (see also Photo 23) Notice the mare's "tucked in" chin, and the mouth open. Observe, too, how short the reins and the fact that the rider has the curb rein even tighter than the snaffle. There is a story along with this picture. Our riders commit practically every other possible fault at one time or another. But because we stress so heavily the fact that a horse *must have* the freedom of his head and neck to jump decently, we had to go back seven years to find a photo to illustrate the point! Photo #23, where the same fault is present to a very slight degree, is also an old picture.

Ruffle through the entire book, and you will observe that practically every photo shows a horse jumping with extended head and neck. Even in Photo #26, where a real dilemma has developed (which will be discussed later) obviously the pony is not *in the habit* of being "caught in the mouth." Instead of over-bending at the poll and tucking in the chin as a horse who has become *accustomed* to insufficient rein over the fence will, this pony looks as shocked as his rider!

Remember that we *demand* that our riders jump with loose reins, catching the mane until they are very secure over fences. The free, confident style of jumping the horses demonstrated on the pages of this book show the result of this method.

Photo by Howard Allen, Middleburg, Va.

PHOTO 13

Fault 13. *Seat too far out of the saddle.* This photo shows another twelve-year-old pupil whose style is far from established; most of the time she still should—and does—catch mane, elementary fashion. Notice that she straightens her leg too much, thus making it impossible for the knee to fit in to the knee roll. (Observe what happened in another picture when she attempts to "follow.")

Photo by Howard Allen, Middleburg, Va.

PHOTO 14

Fault 30. *"Lopsided"*—Rider looks to the right; both hands are on the right: balance is off to the right.

Photo by Howard Allen, Middleburg, Va.

Photo 15

Fault 21. *Feet on the outside of the stirrup.* (See also photo #7.) This photo shows a reasonably good overall "design"; the rider should be stepping down on the insides of her stirrup to be sure, but she does have the stirrups functioning as a floor under her, from which to "step and spring." However, there is still the needless piece of iron to hit the horse in the sides. ("Intermediate to advanced" style.)

Fault 25. *Feet "East and West."* This picture illustrates the rider with her heels rolled in and her toes rolled out, and in addition, as pointed out above, her feet fail to step on the insides of her stirrups. In spite of the poor behavior of her feet, this particular rider, with long and supple legs, does manage to keep her knees in place, which becomes something of a feat!

Photo by Howard Allen, Middleburg, Va.

PHOTO 16

Fault 14. *Seat that does not "clear the saddle" during the jump.* Remember that the horse is best able to jump boldly and freely if the rider relieves him of all the weight he can without, of course, sacrificing his own security or control. While in the picture illustrating this fault the fence is so low that no great effort and freedom of the horse's back is demanded, the rider needs to master this technique in the early stages of jumping, so that it will be a firm habit when the fences are big. Many a hind knock-down has been brought about by the rider coming down on the horse's loins. (Essentially beginning-intermediate style.)

Fault 8. *Hands too low.* (see also photo #8) The rider has "dropped" both her hands and her seat; legs have slipped slightly forward, letting her down on her horse.

Photo by Howard Allen, Middleburg, Va.

PHOTO 17

Fault 9. *Hands that "break" backwards at the wrist.* The rider is bending her wrists backwards in such a way that they could not possibly be pulled forward by the movement of the horse's head and neck in the soft, free gesture of good contact. I'm afraid we can't even blame the bad technique on the interesting obstacles clustered in front of the jump! ("Elementary-Intermediate" style.)

Photo by Howard Allen, Middleburg, Va.

PHOTO 18

Fault 11. *Curb rein too tight.* In the photo shown, the fact that the rider has more "feel" on the curb than on the snaffle is doing no real harm. However, this is a bad habit; it will interfere when the rider attempts to maintain contact and "follow through the air" as the horse certainly will not be eager to "lean" on the curb. This is a young rider (age 12) still jumping on an elementary level. In most respects, her style is quite good.

Fault 2ℂ. *Feet shot "home" (through to the instep) in the stirrups.* (See also photos #6, #9, and #20.)

Fault 22. *Insufficient break inwards—toward the horse—at the ankle.* Doubtless you have spotted the "strange figure from another era." Correct, it is I, some twenty-five years ago. There is more wrong than just the insufficient break at the ankle, although this seemed the most concrete fault upon which to fasten. I was a little bit "behind" (note the fact that the lower leg is *not* back just enough to enable the stirrup leathers to hang *straight* down) and very probably I will come down on the horse's back before he lands. This picture was taken when I still rode what I considered a "Virginia hunting seat" and like many other people I have known since, I would insist: "but I ride forward over fences." Somehow, it never comes out 100% right in such cases!

I might add that I would skin any of my pupils whom I found jumping without a hard hat! (Intermediate style.)

Photo by Budd Studio, New York, N.Y.

Photo 20

Fault 10. *Hands that "break" the straight line of action to the horse's mouth by rounding of the wrists.* As we commented in the discussion of this fault, hands that break the straight line from bit to elbow by rounding the wrists generally are soft hands. This is the case here.

Also, our panel thought it interesting that the rider could sit as well as he does and *function* as well as he does on the "outgrown" 11:2 pony. (This was a "last ride" on the small pony; you will see this rider again on a mount of more appropriate size.)

Fault 23. *Feet shot "home" (through to the instep) in the stirrup.* (See also Photos #6, #9, and #18.) Not only is the foot shot "home" but instead of lying flat on the tread as it should, it lies against the side of the stirrup.

43

Photo by Howard Allen, Middleburg, Va.

PHOTO 21

Fault 24. *Feet having toes only on the tread of the stirrups.* It is too bad that the upright post partially obscures the rider's foot. However, you can see that only the toe is in the stirrup, which, most of the time will result in an unsteady leg. Note that the stirrup leather slants slightly forward, leaving a triangle of daylight between it and the rider's leg.

This is one of the two pictures which we "staged." I strongly suspect that the rider's right foot lies in the stirrup properly or I doubt very much that he would have as secure a position as he demonstrates!

Photo by Howard Allen, Middleburg, Va.

PHOTO 22

Fault 5. Arms that "flip out" at the elbows. In the illustration, this fault is doing no great harm, although it certainly looks inelegant! However, it is very unlikely that soft, relaxed wrist joints and hence soft contact with the horse's mouth can be present.

Fault 17. *"Floating lower leg."* This picture, as you probably guessed, was "staged"; it illustrates the point so well that I am sure no additional comments are necessary!

Photo by Howard Allen, Middleburg, Va.

PHOTO 23

Fault 4. *Hands and arms that do not "give" enough over fences.* (see also photo #12) The angle of this pony's head suggests that he may have become accustomed to jumping without quite enough rein. However, the fault of insufficient rein is present to a very slight degree.

Fault 20. *Heels up.* (See also photo #26.) We selected this picture, taken several years ago, since it demonstrates the point particularly well. Notice that the rider, probably as a result of being on her tip toes, has let her leg slip back a little. In general, the photo shows rather nice intermediate style.

Photo by Howard Allen, Middleburg, Va.

PHOTO 24

Fault 6. *Hands that tend to "ball up into tight little fists."* This rider looks as if her determined attitude has resulted in closing her hands into hard fists that certainly lack softness. She is steadying herself on the horse's neck, elementary to intermediate fashion. Body design, excellent.

Photo by Howard Allen, Middleburg, Va.

PHOTO 25

Fault 3. *Back rounded.* As this rider rounds her back, her hands and arms cannot swing forward in a free gesture, and the overall fails to give an impression of alert readiness for future obstacles. We also might expect her to be a little bit unsteady on landing. (Intermediate style of jumping.)

Photo by Howard Allen, Middleburg, Va.

PHOTO 26

Fault 15. *Legs that swing forward.* And now we see *what* happens many times when the legs do swing forward! The pony "stood back and jumped from under her," and to the complete horror of the rider, she was unable to catch up! Incidentally, we took dozens of pictures waiting and hoping for this dramatic second before we caught our victim! (It would be difficult to say what level of riding is demonstrated, since obviously this is not the rider's customary style!)

Fault 20. *Heels up.* (See also photo #23.) As the legs shot forward and the rider lost her correct base of support, her heels almost inevitably came up too.

Fault 27. *Rider too erect.* And note what happens when the rider fails to make the necessary thrust with the body and snaps back!

Fault 32. *"Left behind."* We have already observed the integral parts of this photo and here it is—the long awaited (by the photographer) and shocking (to pony and rider)—L E F T   B E H I N D.

SUMMARY FOR SCORING

Just to be sure that you have not become confused between the cross references (the "see also's . . .") we are summarizing the "Panel's" findings. You can use this page to simplify checking your score.

Fault 1—Head ducking, with rider looking down—Photo 6

Fault 2—Head ducking, to the side—Photo 11

Fault 3—Rounded back—Photo 25

Fault 4—Hands and arms that do not "give" enough over the fence—Photos 12 and 23

Fault 5—Arms that "flip out" at the elbows—Photo 22

Fault 6—Hands that tend to "ball up into tight little fists."—Photo 24

Fault 7—Hands that are too high—Photo 10

Fault 8—Hands too low—Photos 8 and 16

Fault 9—Hands that "break" backwards at the wrist—Photo 17

Fault 10—Hands that "break" the straight line of action to the horse's mouth by rounding of the wrists—Photo 20

Fault 11—Curb rein too tight—Photo 18

Fault 12—Fingers that spread out during the jump—Photo 5

Fault 13—Seat too far out of the saddle—Photo 13

Fault 14—Seat that does not "clear the saddle" during the jump—Photo 16

Fault 15—Legs that swing forward—Photo 26

Fault 16—Legs that swing back—Photo 5

Fault 17—"Floating lower leg"—Photo 22

Fault 18—Knees out—Photo 6

Fault 19—Pivoting on knees—Photos 5 and 7

Fault 20—Heels up—Photos 23 and 26

Fault 21—Feet on the outside of the stirrups—Photos 7 and 15

Fault 22—Insufficient break inwards—toward the horse—at the ankle—Photo 19

Fault 23—Feet shot "home" (through to the instep) in the stirrups—Photos 6, 9, 18, 20

Fault 24—Feet having toes only on the tread of the stirrups—Photo 21

Fault 25—Feet "East and West"—Photo 15

Fault 26—Rider tipped too far forward—Photo 5

Fault 27—Rider too erect—Photo 26

Fault 28—Rider "bracing" in the irons—Photo 9

Fault 29—Rider correct but stiff overall—Photos 4 and 5

Fault 30—"Lopsided"—Photo 14

Fault 31—Rider lying down on hands—Photo 6

Fault 32—Left Behind!—Photo 26

PHOTO SECTION NO. II

Which Is the Best?

The assumption is that you now have a clear picture in your mind of good and bad form over fences. (Remember, this discussion is in relation to the *rider*, not the horse—although the rider's good or bad technique will help or hinder his horse's performance.) In the following group of pictures you will look at three pictures of the same rider, many times taken a few minutes and sometimes even a few seconds apart. Analyze them carefully. While we know that one seldom achieves it, we are taking PERFECTION OF STYLE AND TECHNIQUE as a standard. Many of the points that you will criticize may be doing no great harm in the particular case pictured—but all the same, you should *see* the flaw in form, and avoid it in your own jumping.

There are twelve "sets" of three pictures.

COVER THE TEXT until you make your first, second, and third choices, giving your reasons. Some pictures may be extremely close, stylewise; some are highly controversial, with compensating errors. In these instances, either of two will be accepted as a correct answer. (Remember our "correct answers" are only our opinions—perhaps you will see something in a picture that we missed.)

Deduct nine points if you are in total disagreement with the "Panel" on a particular "set;" six points for a two-thirds disagreement; three points for a one-third disagreement. In this section we feel that a score of 90 or over is EXCELLENT; 80 to 90 GOOD; below 80, do a lot more looking!

Photo by Howard Allen, Middleburg, Va.

PHOTO 27

SET No. 1   First 27; Second 28; Third 29.

In this set, photo 27 was our unanimous choice. The rider is jumping on an elementary level in all three, but with considerable "oomph" and dash in each.

In photo 29 the pony, galloping on with a bit too much zip, took off for his fence early, leaving the little rider to catch up if she could. She is making a valiant effort to compensate for the "left behind" by hanging on to the mane, and leaning forward, but obviously she is badly "left." Notice that her legs have shot forward and she has come down on the pony's back, in contrast to the other two pictures, in which she keeps her feet and legs under her, and her seat clear of the saddle.

In photo 28 she is looking down, and if a quick turn and another fence were close, she would not be in the best position to plan her approach.

Picture 27 is very similar to 28, but in 27 she is "looking where she is going!"

These pictures show an eleven hand pony with a nine year old rider. All in all, she gives an impression of considerable competence and a great deal of determination and spirit.

Photo by Howard Allen, Middleburg, Va.

PHOTO 28

Photo by Howard Allen, Middleburg, Va.

PHOTO 29

Photo by Howard Allen, Middleburg, Va.

PHOTO 31

SET No. 2   First 32; Second 33; Third 31.

There were no differences of opinion about this set of pictures. Take a look at the group for a minute. The photo above obviously is the poorest with the rider off balance and looking down and to the side.

In the lower right the design of body is quite nice and everything is where it belongs (except for the crop!) for a jump at the elementary level.

In the upper right the overall design is good again and this time the rider manages to establish an excellent line of contact from bit to her elbow, and to do so without taking support from the pony's neck. We might criticize the fact that she is dropping her shoulders (or you might say that her seat is a little too high) over a jump of this size.

I know that the crop carried across the withers, giving the impression that it is close to the rider's face, will cause comment. Personally, I feel that a crop can be used more effectively if it is carried straight across the withers rather than down. Naturally, I would like to see it carried *straight* across rather than with its end pointing to the sky, but I do not seriously believe that its smooth side, parallel to the rider's face, is a hazard.

54

Photo by Howard Allen, Middleburg, Va.

PHOTO 32

Photo by Howard Allen, Middleburg, Va.

PHOTO 33

Photo by Howard Allen, Middleburg, Va.

PHOTO 34

SET No. 3   First 36; Second 35; Third 34.

Picture No. 36 is almost a really good jumping photo. In it, the rider is alert, looking ahead, line of torso is good, line from bit to elbow excellent. Her heels are well down and her feet lie exactly where they should be in the stirrups; she seems to have retained contact with the upper calves, and if the lower leg did not swing back, the whole would be excellent.

In photo 35 the design of body and arms is very nice, but if you look closely you will see that she has no contact at all.

In photo 34 the same faults that appear in 35 are present again. In addition, the rider looks down and to the side, and the gesture of her hands and arms is not nearly as good as it is in either photo 35 or 36. In *each* of the three pictures her lower leg swings back. A little more depth of heel and "stepping down" as well as closing in the lower legs might prevent this.

Perhaps you recognize the horse and rider as a pair you met several times in Photo Section 1. Picture 36 was taken at The Washington International Horse Show under lights and with flash bulbs, which accounts for the odd appearance of the horse's eye.

Photo by Howard Allen, Middleburg, Va.

PHOTO 35

Photo by Budd Studio, New York, N. Y.

PHOTO 36

Photo by Howard Allen, Middleburg, Va.

PHOTO 37

SET No. 4   First 39; Second 37; Third 38.

Photo 39 is very nearly a good jumping picture, style-wise. The overall design of the rider's body is good; the line from the bit to her elbow good, and the hands are very soft. Her feet seem to be her trouble spot, as usual; in this case they turn "East and West."

In picture 37 she gets less weight down into her stirrups, sits too much, and hands are not really functioning independently of the rest of her body. There is no real line from bit to elbow. In picture 38, as you can plainly see, things are much worse. She lies down on her hands and catches the mane; clutches with her knees and calves but has no base of support at all—look at the way in which the feet lie in the stirrups, as a result. (Incidentally, this is the second horse we have seen who doesn't fold well over the stone wall with the road block up!)

Photo by Howard Allen, Middleburg, Va.

PHOTO 38

Photo by Howard Allen, Middleburg, Va.

PHOTO 39

Photo by Howard Allen, Middleburg, Va.

PHOTO 40

SET No. 5   First 41; Second 40; Third 42.

We felt that these three pictures should be included for the expressions on the faces of both the horse and rider if for no other reason!

Getting down to serious business, we all agreed that in the picture at top right (41) the rider manages to maintain an excellent line from bit to elbow (although broken very slightly by rounding the wrists), and that her overall design of body is reasonably good.

Second best, we feel, is the picture on this page, above. Again the rider's contact is quite nice but she does straighten her leg too much.

In the third picture, lower right (photo 42) this fault is accentuated even more with the rider standing straight up in her stirrups, thereby sacrificing stability of position (this will probably be more apparent on landing) and destroying the springyness of the hinges of her leg. Once again, she has a rather nice line from bit to the elbow.

These pictures present some other rather interesting angles. This is the rider whom you have seen in earlier pictures and about whom we made the criticism that her hands became "tight little fists with no softness possible." Recently, I have asked her to use the driving hold on the reins and we find that this trick has greatly softened her hands and increased her ability to follow the gestures of the horse's head and neck over a fence. Another interesting point: in all the pictures of this rider taken last summer and fall the position of her feet and legs looked tremendously strong and secure, which is by no means the case in these pictures. The joker in this situation seems to be her newly acquired saddle, into which she does not yet fit very comfortably!

60

Photo by Howard Allen, Middleburg, Va.

PHOTO 41

Photo by Howard Allen, Middleburg, Va.

PHOTO 42

61

Photo by Howard Allen, Middleburg, Va.

PHOTO 43

SET No. 6   First 44; Second 45; Third 43.

We feel that these three photos create an interesting if not a "pretty" panel. The horse's style over fences is not attractive as he has a tendency to "dive." However, his rider does a really excellent job. And now to evaluate: all three pictures show outstanding ability to follow the gestures of the horse's head and neck and at the same time to retain a reasonably good body design. We selected the photo at upper right (photo 44) for the first place inasmuch as the rider sits well *in spite of* her horse. The horse uses his head and neck incorrectly over the fence; this is much more obvious in the "still" photo than it is in action. The rider, by her very smooth style "makes the horse look good" in motion, but the camera reveals exactly what happens. Assuming that there is not much that she can do to *correct* the way he uses himself, once he is in flight, she does the next best thing—leaves him alone, while he is in the air. (In *schooling*, she works on small spreads and triples, taken mainly from a trot to try to correct his bad style—not too successfully as he was eight years old when she bought him, and already "set in his ways.")

In the photo under discussion (44) she "follows" very skillfully. Because the horse reaches out so far with his head, her back looks somewhat rounded as a result of hands and arms being pulled so far forward.

The photo at lower right (photo 45) shows a somewhat more attractive design and again demonstrates excellent contact, but the jump itself is not nearly as difficult. We would like to see the rider get her foot just a hair further into the stirrup—in the same position that it has in the upper picture.

The photo above (photo 43) we placed third since over this easy fence the rider rounds her back slightly and body and legs slip too far forward—almost in front of the saddle. Nor is her following quite as good as it is in the other two photos. Again we would like to see the foot thrust just a little further into the stirrup.

62

Photo by Howard Allen, Middleburg, Va.

PHOTO 44

Photo by Howard Allen, Middleburg, Va.

PHOTO 45

Photo by Howard Allen, Middleburg, Va.

Photo 46

SET No. 7   First 48; Second 46; Third 47. (Photos 48 and 46 may be scored "correct" if reversed)

There was no question about the "bottom of the pile" of these three, but a bit of controversy as to the first and second places. The picture at upper right (Photo 47) shows the least good style—not only on the part of the rider but on the part of the horse. And this time I think that it was the horse's poor jumping form which produced the rider's bad style rather than the other way around. This little horse, who is an excellent field hunter, apparently regarded this three part obstacle with some distrust. He came in, "propped," and looked the situation over before he sprang into the air. The rider's heels came up, she lost her strong base of support, hands flew up a trifle with the displeasing backward bend at the wrists, and quite naturally she lost contact. Also, we must fault the fact that she has permitted her curb rein to become tighter than the snaffle.

Again, it is rather close between first and second but we selected the picture at lower right (Photo 48) for first place since it really shows a higher degree of skill than the picture on this page (Photo 46). In this photo the rider manages to maintain contact without taking any support from the neck and everything else is approximately where it belongs.

The photo above is perhaps the most attractive of the three but here the rider takes a hairbreadth of support from the horse's neck. And once again, she has more feel on the curb than on the snaffle rein; the amount of feel on the two reins should be reversed.

Each rider seems to make one or two persistent mistakes; hers is the tendency to let her lower leg slip slightly back, thus losing depth of heel, and to take too much on her curb rein.

Photo by Howard Allen, Middleburg, Va.

PHOTO 47

Photo by Howard Allen, Middleburg, Va.

PHOTO 48

Photo by Howard Allen, Middleburg, Va.

PHOTO 49

SET No. 8   First 49; Second 50; Third 51. 49 and 50 may be scored "correct" if reversed.

This is one of our "controversial" groups.

First, suppose we take a look at the three. Photo 51 is undoubtedly the poorest of the set. In it, the rider stiffens at the knees, braces in the stirrups and shoots her legs in front of her. There is a feeling of stiffness throughout the picture, although the position of torso is good, and the line from bit to elbow is excellent. In 50 we see a picture that is better, although there is still a suggestion of stiffness at the knee. My feeling is that the lower leg is not in a position to function; that the rider is still standing in the stirrups and that the leg is floating from the knee down. Had we not seen photo 51, in which the stiffness in the lower leg is more apparent, we might not spot the fault in 50. *Technically,* it is almost an excellent jumping picture, and the only specific faults we could find would be that the lower leg should be moved back a bit, the knee joint relaxed, and the calves closed in.

Photo 49 shows other technical errors; the rider takes support from the horse's neck and looks down; the lower leg floats from the knee down. All the same, picture 49 presents so much more clearly a picture of fluid balance and sureness, that it is hands down *my* choice for first place; some of our panel disagree, and place 50 first. We all agreed that when faced with a more difficult obstacle, the rider seems to bend every nerve to move with her horse, and becomes a more able rider. The difference seems to be that in both photo #51 and #50 the rider gives the impression of standing stiffly in the stirrups over the fence while in photo 49 she moves in one piece with the horse.

Photo by Howard Allen, Middleburg, Va.

PHOTO 50

Photo by Howard Allen, Middleburg, Va.

PHOTO 51

Photo by Howard Allen, Middleburg, Va.

PHOTO 52

SET No. 9   First 53; Second 52; Third 54. Photos 52 and 53 may be scored "correct" if reversed.

This set of pictures, I suspect, may be a little deceptive at a casual glance. The pony above is so much more photogenic than the horse shown in the two pictures on the right that it is hard to appraise the three photos realistically. However, let us study the details for a moment. In the picure above (photo 52) the rider demonstrates body design that is strong and excellent throughout. However, of the three pictures this is the only one in which she fails to maintain perfect contact with the horse's mouth from bit to elbow. Observe that the left rein loops up ever so slightly. If I did not know the exact circumstances I would also criticize the fact that the rider is looking to the right. However, she is riding a horse-shoe shaped outside course and even while she is in the air over the jump she is planning and preparing for the next fence.

The photo at upper right (photo 53) is really hard to fault; it shows not only a lovely design of body but perfect following, with hands and arms taking no support from the neck. If we wish to find a fault we might say that we would like a little more depth of heel.

The photo at lower right (photo 54) is quite similar but not as good since this time she rounds her back; and again we would like to see more depth of heel, strengthening the position of the leg.

Now then, I am sure there can be no question as to the fact that the picture at upper right is the best but since we find "compensating faults" in the other two I believe that we would have to accept as "correct" these two rated either way.

Photo by Howard Allen, Middleburg, Va.

PHOTO 53

Photo by Howard Allen, Middleburg, Va.

PHOTO 54

Photo by Howard Allen, Middleburg, Va.

PHOTO 55

SET No. 10   First 55; Second 56; Third 57.

Our "panel" agreed that the placing of these three pictures was fairly clear cut. In the picture at lower right (Photo 57) the rider has a rather good design of body, but it is achieved by clutching the mane. And even with the support of the mane her lower leg has slipped a little out of place.

In the photo at upper right (Photo 56) she attempts to follow and does it reasonably well, but notice that her leg has come away from the side of the saddle. This is an easy fence and she should be able to sit over it without this fault.

In the above photo (Photo 55) we see her riding over a much more difficult fence and the hands and arms are functioning ably and softly. Design of body is more attractive than in the upper right picture although the same fault persists—her knee sits away from the saddle.

One other fault appears in all three photos and apparently it is a besetting sin —in each picture the rider looks slightly down instead of readying herself for the next obstacle.

You might be interested in knowing more about the taking of these three pictures. This rider took her very first jump (at about one foot in height!) just a little more than two years ago. Photos 56 and 57 (also photo 6 in photo section I) were taken about five months ago. Photo 55 was taken approximately four months later, during which time, as the picture shows, the rider has made tremendous progress.

Photo by Howard Allen, Middleburg, Va.

PHOTO 56

Photo by Howard Allen, Middleburg, Va.

PHOTO 57

Photo by Howard Allen, Middleburg, Va.

Photo 58

SET No. 11   First 58; Second 59; Third 60.

In the picture above (Photo 58) we see a rider functioning in a fashion that is essentially correct and workmanlike throughout, over a somewhat bulky spread jump. The "following" is lovely and the overall design of the body good. We might like to see her obtain a little more depth of heel and to get the tread of the stirrup square across under the balls of her feet and at the same time to drop her seat just a little. But these are minor defects in a very ably executed jump.

In the photo at top right (Photo 59) the rider most certainly is straightening her leg excessively—thereby getting her seat much too far out of the saddle, but she is doing such a beautiful job of "following" over a big fence that I find it hard to be too critical. (This is certainly the best job we have seen on the part of the horse over this particular fence at this height!)

Photo #60 isn't nearly as good as either of the other two. In it, the rider makes her customary mistake of getting her seat too far from the saddle and failing to drive her heels down without compensating by the very excellent use of hands and arms that she demonstrated in the other two photos.

Photo by Howard Allen, Middleburg, Va.

PHOTO 59

Photo by Howard Allen, Middleburg, Va.

PHOTO 60

Photo by Howard Allen, Middleburg, Va.

PHOTO 61

SET No. 12   First 61; Second 63; Third 62.

There is no question about the last place here since in one picture the rider exhibits elementary style—although we use the word "elementary" in a different sense than we do when describing the customary style of the ten or twelve year old rider! Obviously, she is very able, and those of us who observed the "picture-taking" know why the left hand is on the mane and the right hand is dropping. The horse she rides is in his first year of serious schooling. He has been brought along slowly and has complete confidence in this rider. However, the barrels on top of the chicken-coop did give him pause and he interrupted his lovely free style of galloping to hesitate for a second and to look the situation over on his approach to the jump. When this occurs it is more or less inevitable that the rider will have to catch the mane.

In photo 63, lower right, we suspect that the horse has made the same sort of fence, and this time the rider very cleverly made a quick thrust with her body, and dropped her arms almost around his neck to stay "with" him. Notice how well she maintains her overall body position in both of these photos.

And then in photo 61, everything came out exactly right. This fence was taken in stride; this time the rider is able to demonstrate essentially flawless style.

PHOTO 62

PHOTO 63

PHOTO SECTION NO. III

The Unphotogenic Seconds

When you go to the horseshow, undoubtedly at least one horse show photographer will be on hand to mark the second when you smilingly receive the lovely challenge trophy bowl offered for the horsemanship finals. He will also send you pictures of yourself and your horse silhouetted against the sky, straight up over the fence. This is the second when you and he look your collective best. You may be sure that he will *not* send pictures of your horse and you on the way to the fence, or in that most awkward (in appearance) moment in the takeoff when the horse "sits" for a split second on his hocks; nor is he likely to perpetuate for you the moment, just before the first hoof strikes the ground in landing, when the horse's head comes upward. For one thing, it is highly unlikely that you will sit your best at these phases of the jump.

All the same, if you are to be a serious student of jumping, you should know not only how your body should behave, but how the horse's body should behave during these unphotogenic seconds.

We are including five pictures of one horse and rider in successive phases of the same jump (these were actually gotten by the rider and horse taking the fence five times); then we will show you another horse and rider who handle the situation slightly differently. Both horse and rider combinations perform well.

Next we will show you some individual pictures of different horses to illustrate some other specific points.

Photo by Howard Allen, Middleburg, Va.

PHOTO 64

This is the last stride before the actual take-off. Notice the manner in which the horse extends her head and neck. She is making preparation for the balancing movements which she will use over the fence itself.

The rider is handling this part of the approach extremely well. She maintains a strong base of support and an alert attitude. This rider manages to establish an excellent, light feel on the bit at the same time that she permits the mare free use of her head and neck.

Photo by Maxine Rude, Arlington, Va.

PHOTO 65

This picture was taken by a different camera and on a different day, but it does show you the same horse and rider a split second later than in photo 64.

Now you see the horse when the forelegs have already left the ground, and the hind legs have moved well under the body. The mare's head comes up and slightly in, as she gathers herself together and prepares for a bold jump.

At this moment, the rider has stiffened a trifle, and, abandoning contact, has lost to some extent, the excellent base of support that she exhibited in picture 64.

Photo by Howard Allen, Middleburg, Va.

PHOTO 66

We do not have in this particular series that split second when the horse "sits" on her hocks, before she prepares to release the "springs" of her body. (This particular point we will show you in one of the individual pictures.) In a sense, there is a picture missing here, as you now see the horse when the "spring" is fully released and the flight is about to begin.

The rider is handling this phase of the jump rather well although she really doesn't need to get quite so far out of the saddle at this point.

Photo by Howard Allen, Middleburg, Va.

PHOTO 67

Here is the apex of the jump. From the relationship of the horse's body to the fence, we judge that her takeoff was somewhat early. The horse's body is functioning well, although there is no indication of any great effort on the part of the horse. In other words, the jump is an easy one for this mare. The whole looks very free, with the horse using well (and permitted the free use of) her head and neck. The rider's hands are good and she moves in one piece with the horse, but she would create the impression of more security and more strength if she had greater depth of heel.

Photo by Howard Allen, Middleburg, Va.

Photo 68

Now you see the last phase of the actual jump, in which the horse's right front prepares to strike the ground. It will be followed by the left front, each of which, in turn, will lift before the hind legs ground.

If the jump were higher, at this second we would see more of an upward gesture of the horse's head and neck, forming a sharper angle with the body.

The rider manages to keep a good base of support although her performance would be bettered by relaxing her arms at the elbows, permitting the proper bend.

Photo by Howard Allen, Middleburg, Va.

PHOTO 69

In this picture you see a horse and rider combination whose style is quite different from that which you have just observed in the 64-68 sequence.

The first horse gallops on and takes the bit willingly. This horse has a very able jump but tends to loaf up to her fences. One wonders if the dual performance would not be bettered by the rider getting the horse on contact and "putting her together" on her approaches. However, in the case of a horse which, approaching thus, still makes a good jump, this rider's method may be the best. Over-riding can often cause more difficulties than under-riding. The rider exhibits great softness and certainly is completely non-disturbing.

This picture will interest you in that it shows one phase of the approach which the others did not—that fraction of a second when the first foreleg has already pushed off; it will be followed by the second almost as (and often a fraction of a second before) the hind legs ground.

Photo by Howard Allen, Middleburg, Va.

PHOTO 70

In this photo you see the horse at a point in the jump that follows the phase you saw in photo 66, and precedes that of photo 67, where the horse was level over the top of the jump. Here the horse is still slightly on the ascent.

The rider performs in a satisfactory manner, although we would like to see her hands and arms move forward somewhat more freely. Probably this would happen if she did not lie down on her horse so far.

PHOTO 71

A very pleasing second in the beginning of the descent, when the horse's front legs have almost unfolded but have not yet snapped out to their full extension as they will before touching the ground. In this picture, the rider's performance is equally as pleasing as that of her horse.

Photo by Howard Allen, Middleburg, Va.

PHOTO 72

Here we are a second later when the horse's left foot is almost ready to ground. This is essentially the same moment that you saw in photo 68. I think the difference in the two horses and riders interesting.

I like the rider's behavior here the better of the two—hands and arms are so much softer and more relaxed. In the first series, horse and rider were bolder, keener and more "connected." (That horse will force her rider to be bold and keen, or else be badly "left.")

In the second series, the rider is more passive, but both horse and rider together are perhaps softer, and a little freer.

Photo by Howard Allen, Middleburg, Va.

PHOTO 73

Now for a look at some of the "separate" special shots.

This horse's manner of jumping suggests that he is on a trampoline. He may "bounce" several times before the fence, bounce way over it, with his tail winding gaily, bounce a bit on landing.

Here, apparently he thought to line up his hind legs (as he should on the take-off itself) a full stride early. He will now put in a rather uncomfortable stride for the rider again ranging his hind legs on one line. Contrast this with the free style demonstrated in photos 64-68 when the horse gallops and jumps in stride.

The rider's attitude is excellent on the approach.

Photo by Homer K. Heller, Falls Church, Va.

Photo 74

Here we see the early phase of the actual take-off. I am including this particular picture for two reasons.

One, it shows the horse who "gallops on" in a fast approach and for this—to him—low fence, he does not line up his hind legs. His jumps tend to be long and flat, as you will note in photos #104 and 110.

Second, I am including this picture because it shows this phase of the jump exceptionally well ridden.

Photo by Homer K. Heller, Falls Church, Va.

PHOTO 75

Here is the same horse and rider at that second that we termed "sitting on the hocks." Observe how much weight goes into the fetlock joints and how much the pasterns bend. Notice here also, the horse has failed to line up his hind legs very accurately.

Again the rider handles this part of the jump well, although this time her legs have slipped a little; hands and arms are extremely nice.

Photo by Homer K. Heller, Falls Church, Va.

PHOTO 76

Here is an excellent example of the horse "basculing." This means the rounding of the horse's back, accompanied by the strong forward and downward thrust of the head and neck at the moment when the front hooves pass over the obstacle. The horse makes himself into a sort of crescent moon. This *should* occur over a difficult fence, and will occur most times over an easy fence, when the horse gets in too close on the take-off. You may also see it in the case of a green horse who finds even a low fence difficult.

Photo by Homer K. Heller, Falls Church, Va.

PHOTO 77

Again you see the horse supported by one foreleg only, in the first phase of the take-off. The picture is included because the attitude and overall design of the rider is particularly good.

Photo by Howard Allen, Middleburg, Va.

Photo 78

Note that, in this picture, instead of continuing the gallop for one more stride, the horse's weight has shifted to his hindlegs; there is no more forward motion. The rider is sitting down and attempting to squeeze; her hands went up on the neck as the horse stopped. I am sure that as you examined the picture, you spotted the refusal!

Photo by Howard Allen, Middleburg, Va.

PHOTO 79

Lastly, you may be interested in seeing the way in which the horse's back, legs, head and neck perform when galloping boldly and jumping well up over a good sized fence. Over this sizable fence (for her—actually this is a 13:1 hand pony) at this phase of the jump, her head and neck move up.

This movement permits, on one hand, the full extension of the forelegs and on the other, the caving in of the back. The latter, in turn, helps to raise the quarters and hind feet as they clear the fence.

Note the two horse show judges standing, cards in their hands, to the left. Observe that the rider is preparing to turn to the left, to follow the circular outside course.

PHOTO SECTION NO. IV

About the Jumps; About the Picture-Taking
About the Following Picture Section

At this point I think the reader might be interested in knowing a little about the actual jumps that we used in our photos.

I am sure that you will have observed that some pictures show riders going over the rustic fences, white poles between wings, chicken-coops, etc., that one is likely to meet in the hunter classes at horseshows. Undoubtedly you have already decided which pictures are horseshow pictures, quite as much from the type of jumps shown as from the fact that in these pictures the horses' manes are braided and in many cases you can see that the rider is wearing a number. In general, these horseshow jumps for the hunter classes are not too interesting.

You must have observed also that the fences that we use at home are quite different, and perhaps you would like to know the reason for this.

All of our horses are hunter type. We feel that if ever there is a horse that should take PRECISELY THE OBSTACLE the rider asks, it is the hunter. If he has to be held to his particular panel or obstacle by wings he is not worth much. The argument on the other side is that in actual hunting, the horse is never asked to take a jump sitting out in the middle of a field. Very true, BUT it is of paramount importance that the horse take the *very panel of rail fence* at which you point him, even though the adjoining panel may be lower! If he attempts to duck out and take the lower panel, he may well cause an accident with another horse and rider. Or if the chicken-coop jump set in a wire fence looks to him like a "wingless" jump, with an easier way around, he will indeed come to grief. Again, *you* may know that there is a bad hole on the left hand side of a fallen log, and your horse must take the higher part of the log on the right. In other words, he must have the confidence in himself and in you to take whatever jump you ask—or he should be left at home. For these reasons, from the very first one foot jump, we never school with wings. (The little rustic wings that you see at the ends of the stone wall jump were put up "just for pretty" when we took pictures.) But we do make every step easy for the horse, allowing him to build up his confidence slowly.

There is another comment that we frequently hear: "But I don't want to make my good show ring hunter all 'crazy' and 'hot' by pushing him over those funny looking jumps! After all, he is a hunter, and he is not supposed to take striped poles."

Who told him that because he would go in show ring hunter classes that he wasn't supposed to jump striped poles? Somebody must have explained to him that the odd looking little white picket gate that he will encounter in hunter classes at Madison Square Garden IS a hunter jump, and that the striped poles are not. He certainly didn't figure this out himself, and explain it to the humans. So at home we tell our hunters, "Look, friend; you jump anything that I point you towards, and on my honor you will never be asked to jump anything that is too big or too difficult for you."

This, in effect, is exactly what you are putting across to your horse by slow, careful schooling. And as long as your judgment of what he can master step by step is intelligent, and your method of riding non-abusive but confident, he will believe you. There is no reason why he should get "hot" and "crazy" because he jumps a variety of obstacles. It is only bad riding and bad schooling that will do this.

And now, having explained the reason that we use the type of jumps that we do at home, perhaps you would like to hear of the way we went about collecting pictures for this book. About twenty or twenty-five per cent of the photos are horse show pictures. Almost all of the rest we acquired in three "picture-taking" days at home. First, on one somewhat grey day last fall we asked our good friend and very excellent cameraman, Howard Allen, to come up from Middleburg and "shoot" about twenty of our riders. From the one-hundred-and-some pictures that he took for us that day, we hoped to reap a real harvest. We counted on these pictures to illustrate almost every fault of jumping, as well as some to show *good* style. For this reason, we used riders at various levels of riding, on both horses and ponies—some excellent jumpers; others more difficult or green.

It turned out well. We found that these, together with the horse show pictures we already had, illustrated nearly every fault we had described.

But then a more critical look convinced us that we had been so engrossed in observing and analyzing WHAT THE RIDER WAS DOING OVER THE FENCE, that our fences themselves were dull and uninteresting. In other words, we had just set up *something* for the horses and ponies to jump over, while we fixed our complete attention on the technique of the riders.

We decided that we could study style just as effectively, and enjoy the book more (and have a lot more fun with our picture-taking), if we took the trouble to set up more of a variety of jumps.

So when the winter snows melted, even before the leaves came out, on the first sunny day, we shot again. You will find most of these pictures in photo sections III, IV, and V, with a sprinkling of them through section II. I hope that you will agree with me that the book becomes more interesting by the use of a less standard type of jumps.

Then we studied our pictures a little longer and harder. Something was missing. Shouldn't the readers know how both horse and riders function on the approach to a jump, and in the early unphotogenic phases and on the descent, as well as in that classic second at the apex of the jump when horse and rider are outlined against the sky? Once again, and at the eleventh hour, Howard Allen dropped everything and dashed up from Middleburg. From about sixty pictures taken that day we did get enough to show you almost every phase of the approach and of the jump itself. These pictures, of course, you found in photo section III.

Now, in Photo Section IV, we present a group of pictures almost all of which are good; many are excellent. Purposely we have included, in this section, pictures of fences ridden *well* at an elementary level by young children on ponies, to emphasize once again that a good job can be done at each stage of riding ability. Obviously, a good job at an elementary level is quite different from a good job at an advanced level. And let me hasten to add that not *all* of the "pony riders" are "young children." Some are very able teen-age riders who ride their fourteen hand ponies in a highly skillful manner. The latter part of this section shows you riders mounted on horses, as opposed to ponies.

In this photo section you will find twenty-five pictures. This type of section will be difficult to score, but if you wish to do the section as a quiz, cover the text, and make your evaluation. If you are in *total* disagreement with the book, on any photo, deduct four points. Deduct a proportionate fraction for partial disagreements. Or just read our evaluation and decide if you agree or disagree.

Photo by Howard Allen, Middleburg, Va.

PHOTO 80

Sherrill Milnor on *Sauce Box*

This photo demonstrates lovely elementary style. In spite of catching the mane, this little rider most assuredly interferes in no way with the pony's ability to use himself freely. Everything is exactly where it belongs; I particularly like the fact that she looks up and is ready to plan for her next fence. This picture is an excellent example of the young rider on a small pony who does everything well at her particular level of riding.

How much more satisfactory to observe her than it would be if she were attempting *unsuccessfully* to follow the gestures of the pony's head and neck!

Photo by Howard Allen, Middleburg, Va.

PHOTO 81

Susan Bishop on *Strawman*

Good elementary style. This young rider creates an impression of considerable elegance at the elementary level. If she had managed to keep her seat off the pony until after landing, we would have to say "perfect at the elementary level." (This is the same pony you saw in another section with legs tightly folded. He has a great deal of natural jumping ability, but a lazy temperament. As a result he loafs up to his fences and jumps so slowly that it is hard to retain good style on him.)

Photo by Howard Allen, Middleburg, Va.

PHOTO 82

Sally Jones on *Result*

This picture demonstrates nice style at the elementary level. If we wish to criticize we might say that the rider could use more depth of heel and consequently clear the saddle a little further; that she is looking slightly to the right instead of straight between the pony's ears, and that the left hand, which does not catch the mane, has become a little stiff in the wrist.

Photo by Homer K. Heller, Falls Church, Va.

PHOTO 83

Randy Dillon on *Bela*

Here we have a photo of another elementary rider taken from a somewhat unusual angle.

The rider shows good style and timing at his level, with the heels well down, legs closing in, over-all design satisfactory, and head up, alert and ready for the next fence.

Photo by Howard Allen, Middleburg, Va.

PHOTO 84

Joe Fargis on *Cymro Bach*

Here we see once again, the rider on the "outgrown" pony, coping with an awkward situation with considerable ease. In spite of his rounded back, his right leg slipped too far behind the girth, and his left rein looping, the very soft use of his hands and his ability to stay "all in one piece" with the small pony is impressive.

This would have to be considered intermediate to advanced style.

Photo by Homer K. Heller, Falls Church, Va.

PHOTO 85

Laurie Kahn on *Fairlad*

Here we have another "pony rider" handling a somewhat formidable fence in a creditable style. She is able to make a good effort to follow although she takes some support from the pony's neck, and the hands could be softened a bit. We would like to see her get more depth of heel with more bend at the ankle, and more angle at the knee. In other words, she should step down in the stirrups just a little more, thereby bringing her seat closer to the saddle.

The fence is ridden in essentially intermediate style.

Photo by Howard Allen, Middleburg, Va.

PHOTO 86

Judy Triebel on *Misty*

This rider demonstrates a pleasing over-all design, good timing and a keen attitude toward the future.

She is handling the fence in excellent intermediate style.

Photo by Howard Allen, Middleburg, Va.

PHOTO 87

Nancy Hahn on *Brigadoon*

This time we have a young teen-age rider on a tremendously bold-jumping large pony. The rider looks as keen and alert as her mount and there is no doubt that both know exactly what they are doing. If we are to criticize, it would be to say that the photo gives us the impression that the rider is a little stiff and that she may have "flipped forward" somewhat abruptly. Also her feet are not lying quite squarely in her stirrups. She achieves an excellent line from bit to elbow and the fact that she takes support from the neck cannot really be criticised in riding over solid fences on an outside course.

The fence is ridden in good intermediate style.

Photo by Peter Grant, Washington, D. C.

PHOTO 88

Jackie Heller on *Little Nibs*

Here we have a pony and rider combination that we think most pleasing to observe. She not only gives the impression of being capable and knowing exactly where she is going, but she combines these qualities with excellent technique. I particularly like the very strong and secure seat and legs. The only criticism that we find might be that she is taking support from the neck, although she establishes a good line of action from bit to elbow, broken upwards only a hair's breadth. While from a practical point of view over hunter jumps there is no objection to this, she does place the jump in intermediate ranks by so doing.

Photo by Howard Allen, Middleburg, Va.

PHOTO 89

Joe Fargis on *Misty*

Again you meet a rider whom you have seen several times before, this time on a mount of more appropriate size. The part which impresses me is his ability to "get with" his mount, maintaining both security and softness. We might like to see him get a little more bend at the ankle-joint so that his feet would fit flat against the tread of the stirrups. We might like to see him drop his seat a little closer to the saddle to create a stronger position. In spite of these faults the "fluid" quality of this style over fences is quite outstanding.

The style is essentially advanced.

Photo by Budd Studio, New York, N. Y.

PHOTO 90

Nan Wood on *Little Nibs*

I consider this one of the few examples of flawless style over a fence. However, there has been some controversy on this point. The criticism, if any, seems to be that the rider's reins are a little long; that if she would shorten her reins a hair, the arms could and would swing forward more freely. My contention is that for the height of the fence (3′) and in consideration of the short pony neck, her reins are exactly the right length. If she shortened the reins to any great extent she would find herself hugging the pony around the neck. If again, this fence were 4′ instead of 3′, requiring the pony to reach out in a strong gesture, the rider's hands would be pulled further forward. I feel that the line which she has established from bit to elbow is perfect. It is soft and yet the whole gives a feeling of complete efficiency. The rider's heels are down, the stirrup leathers are hanging vertical, her seat just clears the saddle, her back is hollow, she is looking up and is completely absorbed in the performance of her mount and in planning the ride. To me, this picture demonstrates able and lovely style.

This fence is ridden on an advanced level.

Photo by Howard Allen, Middleburg, Va.

PHOTO 91

Bev Hink on *Mighty John*

This rider gives the impression of riding ably and securely. She has an excellent base of support and good design of body; the over-all is marred by the fact that she turns her head to the side, flips her elbows out and leans on her hands.

In this attractive picture the rider is using elementary-to-intermediate technique.

Photo by Howard Allen, Middleburg, Va.

PHOTO 92

Peggy Hahn on *Little Minx*

Not only does this young rider demonstrate an over-all design of body and legs that is correct and works well, but she suggests a very "live and fluid" style of jumping. She takes support from the horse's neck, thereby placing herself in intermediate ranks, but presents excellent style and technique at that level.

Photo by Howard Allen, Middleburg, Va.

PHOTO 93

Mary Lou Walsh on *Little Minx*

This very nice picture fails to make "excellent" only because the rider tilts too far forward. If she had settled down into the saddle a bit and driven the heels down I am sure that the over-all would have been near to perfect. Tipped forward as she is, her legs slip back a little and she finds it necessary to steady herself on her hands. In spite of this, she gets a very nice line from bit to elbow, and certainly looks very much "with" her mare.

The rider demonstrates very pleasing intermediate technique.

Photo by Howard Allen, Middleburg, Va.

PHOTO 94

Jill Ridgely on *War Echo*

In spite of certain obvious criticisms, this is a very ably ridden fence. The rider's feet and legs are excellent. If she had not dropped her shoulders so low and rounded her back slightly we would have an outstanding picture. Even though she is flattening out too much, she *is* looking up and planning her ride. Hands are very soft and she is obtaining an excellent line from bit to elbow.

It is in essence such a good performance at high-intermediate level that it is hard to be too critical of the obvious flaw in style.

Photo by Howard Allen, Middleburg, Va.

PHOTO 95

Corky Wells on *My Adventure* — Essentially flawless style.

Photo by Peter Grant, Washington, D. C.

PHOTO 96

Jackie Heller on *Just Willie*

In this photo we see a rider demonstrating the same strong and excellent base of support which she displayed on the pony in photo #82. Placing the two pictures side by side, I am inclined to feel that her leg position is not quite as good in this picture as it is in the other; here, I believe, that the over-all would be bettered if she dropped her stirrups one notch. Her hands too, are similar but not quite as good this time; she seems to be supporting herself on her hands and arms to some extent, rather than permitting them to swing forward freely.

The picture shows, however, a jump ably ridden on an intermediate level with no drastic faults.

Photo by Howard Allen, Middleburg, Va.

PHOTO 97

Sarah Willis on *Blue Wasp*

The above photo shows a pleasing and able style. There has been a little controversy about the lower leg, which may have slipped back a hair. More depth of heel would remedy this. Hands and arms are soft and function well. The rider has flipped her elbows out ever so slightly and is taking a little support from the sides of the horses neck, which, from a practical point of view, does not lessen the efficiency of the performance.

The over-all presents a picture of fluid sureness with the rider using very polished intermediate technique.

Perhaps we should remind the reader that we are using the term "intermediate" in an arbitrary fashion. When the rider takes a little support from the horse's neck, instead of following through the air, we term that particular jump "intermediate," even though the rider obviously is capable of "advanced" technique.

Photo by Howard Allen, Middleburg, Va.

PHOTO 98

Lee Hilts on *One Too Many*

This photo shows a well executed jump with nothing seriously wrong. The rider is following the gesture of the horse's head through the air with her left hand; about the right, we cannot be completely sure. The left hand has dropped a trifle low, but from a practical point of view, there can be no real criticism.

This is a well ridden fence in which the rider uses essentially advanced technique.

Photo by Peter Grant, Washington, D. C.

PHOTO 99

Christine Sieminski on *My Adventure*

This photo shows near-to-perfect jumping style. If we wish to "strain at a gnat" we can say that her legs have slipped back (but just barely); some of us might say that she doesn't need to "lie down" quite so far and that as a result she rounds her back and breaks the straight line from bit to elbow upwards, just a hair.

However, in general, the picture shows a rider who is capable, secure and demonstrates excellent "advanced" technique.

Photo by Howard Allen, Middleburg, Va.

PHOTO 100

Judy Corcoran on *Northblen*

Here we see a rider whose physical build results in suggesting a less strong, secure over-all position than the long legged riders manage to conjure up! Perhaps this could be remedied by having the lower leg brought back a hair. The photo shows a rider with lovely fluid balance, and very soft hands that function beautifully.

This is a well executed jump on the advanced level.

Photo by Howard Allen, Middleburg, Va.

PHOTO 101

Sherry Lough on *Northblen*

This rider's hands and arms function softly and well, but once again we must fault the fact that she very slightly "flies out of the saddle" (knees lose their contact with the flap of the saddle) over the jump. And in addition, once again, we must criticize the fact that she still looks down.

Here the rider demonstrates technique bordering on advanced.

One other point will interest you in connection with this rider. You may have noticed that in Photo Section IV (where you will find the last pictures we shot), she managed to correct these faults. After studying the pictures of herself she vowed that she would not "fly away" over her fences and look down, and sure enough, that day, she didn't!

Photo by Howard Allen, Middleburg, Va.

PHOTO 102

Ridgely Rider on *Twink's Best*

This most attractive photo shows an ably ridden jump. The rider looks strong and secure; in addition, the very soft use of the hands is impressive. She is taking a hairbreadth of support from the neck and one might wish to see the hands and arms swing forward a little more freely. However, horse and rider are functioning so well together, with the rider both strong and soft at the same time, that criticism seems superfluous.

An exceptionally well ridden fence in which the rider demonstrates top-intermediate style.

Photo by Howard Allen, Middleburg, Va.

PHOTO 103

Marion Lee on *Trademark*

The style demonstrated in this photo is so strong, lovely and secure that we do seem to be "straining at a gnat" when we call attention to the very slight slack in the right rein!

This photo provides an excellent example of essentially advanced technique.

PHOTO 104

Nan Wood on *Devil's Bliss*

Here again we see the near-to-flawless style which this rider has demonstrated on various mounts throughout the book. Again, the only very slight criticism is that she should get a little more depth of heel.

This is an excellent example of advanced technique.

PHOTO SECTION NO. V

Line Up Your Winners!

Inasmuch as the "Panel" has done quite a lot of evaluating up to this point, we will now take a holiday, and leave you to do your own analyses. You will "judge" along with two very popular equitation judges.

We have selected ten photos of ten different riders over the same fence. In some, things very obviously are not going quite right for the rider. Some are excellent by any standards. Now, our staff has discussed the style of our riders so much that we already know that so-and-so tends to let her lower leg slip back, and another pupil frequently tightens the curb rein a little too much; another lets her knee slip out of proper position and another pinches too tightly with the knee; somebody else loses contact and somebody else fails to get sufficient depth of heel, and so forth. So this time, instead of our own staff members, we asked two American Horseshow Association Hunter Seat Equitation Judges to line up the class first through tenth.

They were asked to judge on the basis of what they saw at this particular phase of the jump; which rider demonstrated the best technique and the highest degree of skill in the situation in which he found himself when the camera clicked. Judging was done by secret ballot, and no reasons were asked for—just the results.

Look through the section of ten photos, and write down your decisions. Then compare your results with those listed at the end of this section.

PHOTO 105

PHOTO 106

Photo 107

Photo 108

125

PHOTO 109

PHOTO 110

PHOTO 111

PHOTO 112

PHOTO 113

PHOTO 114

DECISIONS OF THE JUDGE

If you have ever been to a horse show you must have heard some parent commenting in a strained voice, "Well really, I just could not follow the way that class was judged! How could they pin that child third over our Peggy?" Undoubtedly, this parent, if she happens to know anything at all about judging horsemanship, saw all the good things that Peggy does—perhaps Peggy makes nice approaches but collapses a bit over fences; perhaps Peggy maintains a good design of body but resorts to catching mane to do so; perhaps Peggy cuts a very nice figure but rides with a fixed hand; perhaps Peggy has a great deal of style but is stiff throughout and comes down on her horse's back in landing.

And perhaps some of a hundred other faults occurred. Now the judges may have had the difficult task of trying to decide whether they preferred the performance of the rider who misfigured one fence but rode the rest of her course very ably, or the rider whose performance was nowhere outstanding but nowhere bad. In other words, it is entirely possible that the judge saw all sorts of faults in the riders whom he pinned as well as faults in those whom he did not pin. He has to decide which out of all the riders committing many compensating errors he ranks as having a better performance. This is one of the reasons why we have asked two people who are very capable horsemanship judges to line up the ten riders whom you too have just judged. We do this to help you to realize that even amongst knowledgeable individuals there will be some divergence of opinion. So don't feel that you have been "robbed" even though your performance went unnoted on a particular day; another day, riding just the same way, the strong points of your performance may be recognized.

If you can do so tactfully, you should try to find out what the particular weak points of your ride were, in the opinion of that particular judge. Perhaps you will even get some conflicting opinions but don't let this worry you either; eventually it will all add up.

RESULTS OF THE LINE UP

First place	No. 110	First place	No. 110
Second place	No. 114	Second place	No. 114
Third place	No. 107	Third place	No. 107
Fourth place	No. 106	Fourth place	No. 104
Fifth place	No. 113	Fifth place	No. 108
Sixth place	No. 104	Sixth place	No. 109
Seventh place	No. 112	Seventh place	No. 113
Eighth place	No. 108	Eighth place	No. 112
Ninth place	No. 111	Ninth place	No. 106
Tenth place	No. 109	Tenth place	No. 111

Judged by: Miss Fen Kollock, Director and Owner of Pegasus Stable, Chevy Chase, Maryland. Recognized Judge AHSA in Hunter Equitation. Chairman elect of the Riding Committee of the DGWS, a branch of the National Education Assn.

Judged by: Mrs. Carol Bailey Miller, Recognized Judge AHSA, Hunter Equitation.

Now, I should like to add that, after the first three places, about which we largely agreed, my "judging" of this group came out rather differently. (My biggest disagreement is in reference to Photo No. 111 which I place *much* higher.) I have the highest respect for the acumen of the two people who "judged" for us. The fact that we differed in evaluating what we saw does not mean that any of the three of us failed to see the same strong or weak points of each rider as presented in the picture.

What it does mean is that inevitably each person will attribute greater or lesser importance to the same quality.

Remember this when you enter your horsemanship event at a horse show!

A NARROW SEGMENT

Before closing this book there is an important point which you must understand.

As I told you in the beginning, I would present just one aspect of an extremely wide topic—the form and style of the rider OVER THE FENCE ONLY (during that time when, the horse having left the ground, the rider can do little to help, but much to hinder) which will permit the horse the maximum opportunity to use his body freely, without the rider's loss of his own security or ability to introduce control—when needed again. (Once the horse is in the air, control becomes a negligible factor.)

Now, this is different from a consideration of the combined factors that result in obtaining *good performances* throughout a course of jumps. In order to produce this good performance in the horse *over the fence,* that horse must have been brought to the most advantageous line of take-off at the correct speed and with the correct amount of impulse—and this must be true at every fence throughout the course.

You have just completed a study of the basic part of jumping. You have observed in considerable detail the way the rider should behave over the fence. This is the *foundation* on which you will build your later skill in negotiating entire courses. The flawless form we have discussed should be *automatic* before you attempt to go further. Then, having mastered the elements of "Form Over Fences" you should be ready to proceed to my next book, which will deal with "Riding Courses for Peak Performance."

Photo 115